PSALM SONGS 2

Lent – Holy Week – Easter

Edited by David Ogden and Alan Smith

CASSELL

Cassell
Wellington House, 125 Strand, London WC2R 0BB

Compilation and editorial material © Cassell plc, 1998

First published 1998

British Library Cataloguing-in-Publication Data
A catalogue record for this book is available from the British Library.

ISBN 0-304-70343-5

Psalm Songs 1	ISBN 0-304-70342-7
Psalm Songs 3	ISBN 0-304-70344-3
Set of three volumes	ISBN 0-304-70345-1
Psalm Songs CD	ISBN 0-304-70335-4
Psalm Songs 1 (5-pack)	ISBN 0-304-70346-X
Psalm Songs 2 (5-pack)	ISBN 0-304-70347-8
Psalm Songs 3 (5-pack)	ISBN 0-304-70348-6
Set of three volumes (5-pack)	ISBN 0-304-70349-4

Music and text typeset by Alan Smith

Printed and bound in Great Britain by Redwood Books, Trowbridge, Wiltshire

Contents

Dedicated to the memory of
Geoffrey Boulton Smith

Introduction

The idea for these three volumes of *Psalm Songs* was first conceived in 1994 by Geoffrey Boulton Smith, then Director of Music for the Roman Catholic Diocese of Portsmouth. Geoffrey had spent much of his life composing and encouraging others to compose music for the liturgy, especially since the reforms of the Second Vatican Council. After his untimely death in 1996 we undertook to complete the project.

The original plan was to provide a responsorial song setting of the psalm for each of the Sundays and principal feast days in both the Roman Lectionary and the Revised Common Lectionary (as adopted by the Church of England in *Calendar, Lectionary and Collects*). In the event it proved impossible to find suitable settings of every one of these psalms, but all the commonly used texts have been included. We have used the Hebrew psalm numbers rather than those in the Greek Septuagint. So, for example, 'The Lord is my shepherd' appears as the twenty-third psalm, and not as the twenty-second.

The psalms are the prayer book of the Bible – the human expression of dialogue between the people of Israel and their God. From the earliest times, a singer was engaged in the synagogues to minister at the scrolls and to lead the psalm singing. They would stand before the ark of the scrolls and intone the liturgy – a leader of prayer on behalf of the assembly. The psalm is a personal response to the Word of God and so today is most suitably placed after the first reading in a eucharistic celebration. In recent years psalm singing has been given fresh impetus by the use of responsorial settings which give scope for solo cantors and choirs, and for the congregation to engage in dialogue with them. *Psalm Songs* brings together 79 such settings, all but two of which have a congregational refrain. (The two exceptions may be sung in their entirety by the congregation.)

There are various ways in which you can help and encourage your congregation to take a full and active part in the singing of these psalms:

- duplicate the congregational refrains which are printed at the back of the books onto your service sheet.
- arrange for a cantor to stand in full view of the people and discreetly indicate when they should sing.
- do not overwhelm your congregation with new material every Sunday. The *common psalms* in the Roman Lectionary will often do duty for several consecutive weeks.
- a short congregational practice before the celebration begins will instil confidence – but don't annoy your people by having one every Sunday.

Some of these settings may be too long or too elaborate for your needs; if so, save them for that 'big occasion' and use a simpler tone or chant setting. This is especially true of the Liturgy of the Word / Ministry of the Word at the principal service on Sundays, where the psalm should reflect on the readings rather than dominate. Some of these settings might be more appropriate at other times in the service: as the entrance song, during communion or as a conclusion to the celebration. Again, those congregations that communally celebrate the Prayer of the Church (in whatever form) will find much here to aid their worship.

Many of the pieces in *Psalm Songs* are published here for the first time. They have all been composed by musicians working in churches today, and they encompass a wide range of contemporary musical styles. In performance the songs should have a sense of growth, with the optional parts for choir and instruments being used to colour or embellish the vocal parts rather than providing a wash of sound, and then only after the congregation can confidently sing the refrain.

We would like to express our thanks to those who have helped us see Geoffrey Boulton Smith's vision through to its fulfilment: the members of the Composers' Group of the Society of Saint Gregory (many of whom are represented in these pages), our wives Lucy and Pauline, and above all Ruth McCurry from Cassell for her commitment, guidance and enthusiasm for this project.

We hope that *Psalm Songs* will find a home in your church and help to make the Word of God live in the hearts of your congregation.

David Ogden & Alan Smith

I Will Leave This Place

Psalm 51

Paul Wellicome

VERSES: *Choir/Cantor*

1. Have mer-cy, ten-der God, for-get that I de-fied you.

2. Cre - at - or, re-shape my heart. Stead-y my spir - it, Lord. Do not

3. Lord, give me words—— and I will shout your praise. So I

Wash a - way my sin, cleanse me from my guilt. I will

cast me from your side, stripped of your Ho - ly Spir - it. I will

of - fer my shat-tered spir - it; a changed heart you wel - come. I will

O Lord, You Love Sincerity Of Heart

Psalm 51

Elizabeth Rees

faults. O wash a-way my___ guilt and pu-ri-fy me from my___ sin. For I

tru-ly know my faults; my sin is con-stant-ly in mind. I have

sinned a-gainst you a - lone. I have done e-vil in your sight.

D.S.

VERSE 2: *Cantor/Choir*

2. O pu-ri-fy me till I am clean, O___ wash me whit-er than the snow. In-

stil in-to me joy and glad-ness; let my bones which you crushed dance for

joy. Turn your eyes a-way from my faults, and wipe a-way all__ my__

guilt. Cre-ate a clean heart for me, O God. Give me a new and con-stant spir-it.

VERSE 3: *Cantor/Choir*

3. Do not ban-ish me__ from your pres-ence; do not de-prive me of your Ho-ly

10

Spir-it. Be my sav-iour a-gain, re-new my joy, keep my spir-it stead-y and

will-ing. O— save me from death, God my help-er, and I will pro-claim— your—

good-ness. Lord, o-pen my lips, and my— mouth will speak your praise.

D.S.

D.S.

Song Of Blessing

Psalm 91

John Glynn

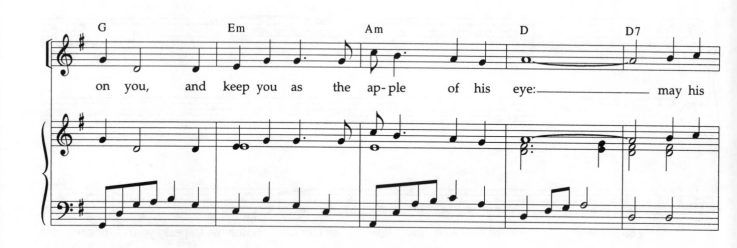

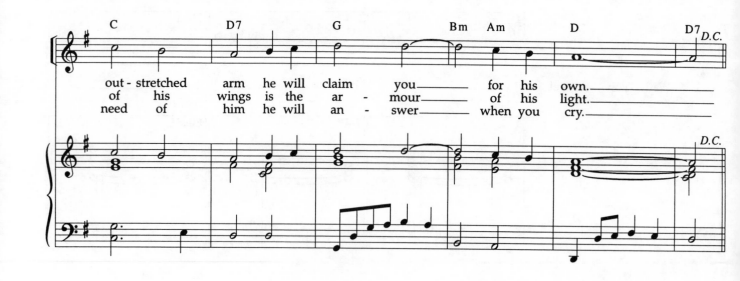

out - stretched arm he will claim you____ for his own.____
of his wings is the ar - mour____ of his light.____
need of him he will an - swer____ when you cry.____

Rest Your Love

for Liz and Eddie

Psalm 33

David Ogden

VERSES: *Choir/Cantor*

O Lord, gently rest your love.

Lord, How Can I Repay

Psalm 116

John Glynn

Final

(D) / F
(Asus4) (A) / Csus4 C
(D) / F

Fine

name, and I will call on your ho - ly name.

VERSES: *Cantor*

(D) / F
(A) / C
(Bm) / Dm

1. I ___ trust - ed, went on trust - ing through the night of
2. In the serv - ice of your peo - ple I will spend my
3. You un - bound me, gave me free - dom: you I glad - ly
4. In the serv - ice of your peo - ple I will spend my

(F♯m) / Am
(G) / B♭
(D) / F

pain; in my an - guish and af - flic - tion
days, giv - ing free - ly of my life - blood
serve. In thanks - giv - ing I will of - fer
days, in your tem - ple, in your Church, Lord,

19

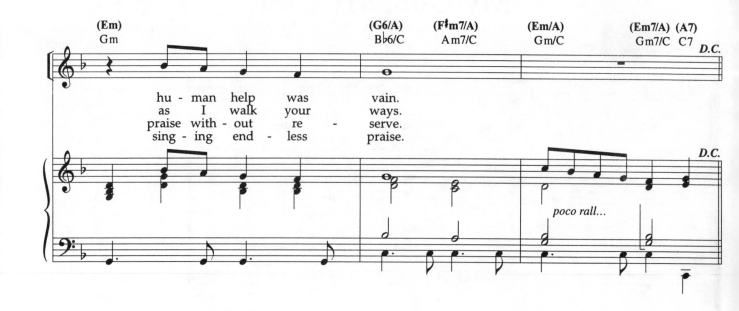

human help was vain.
as I walk your ways.
praise with-out re - serve.
sing-ing end - less praise.

By The Waters Of Babylon

Psalm 137

Traditional

By_____ the wa - ters, the wa - ters of Ba - by - lon

we sat down and wept,___ and wept___ for thee, Zi - on.

We re-mem-bered, we re-mem-bered, we re-mem-bered thee, Zi - on.

Keyboard

Text and music: traditional

20

My God, My God

Psalm 22

Alan Smith

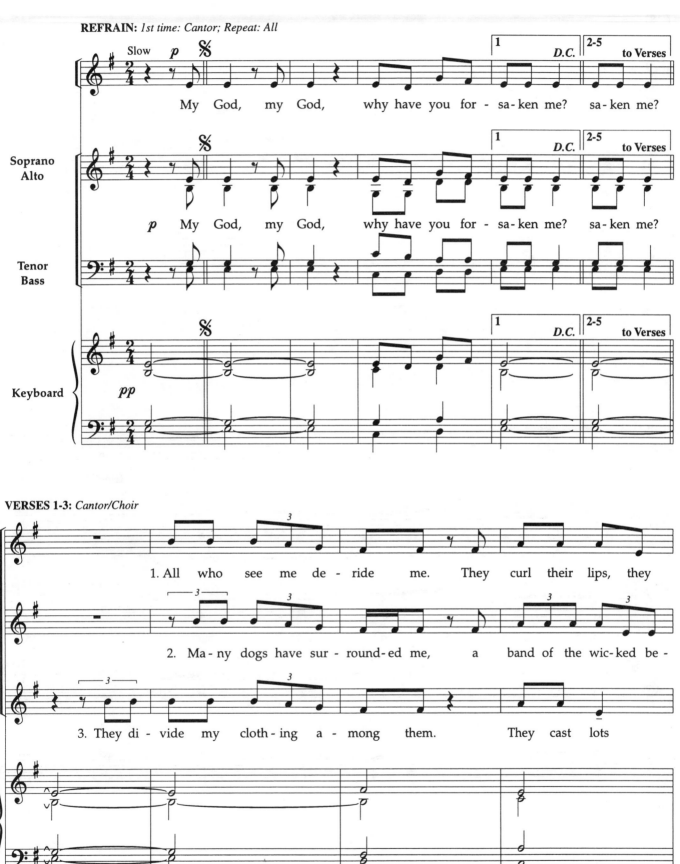

toss their heads. "He trust-ed in the Lord, let him save him;

set me. They tear holes in my hands and my feet.

for my robe. O Lord, do not leave me a-lone, my

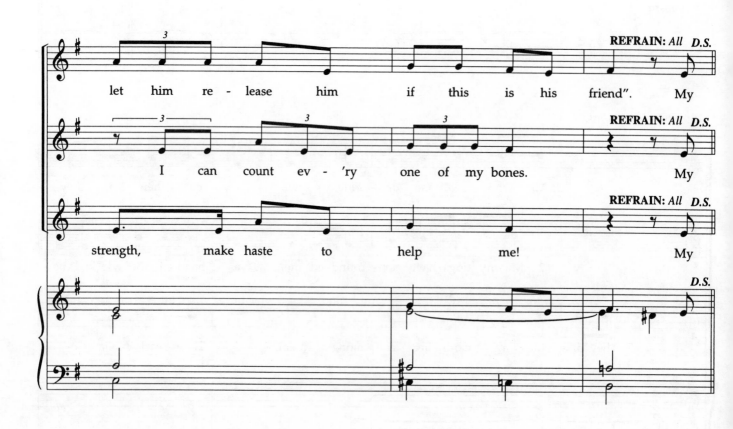

let him re-lease him if this is his friend". My

I can count ev-'ry one of my bones. My

strength, make haste to help me! My

VERSE 4: *Cantor/Choir*

4. I will tell of your name to my peo-ple and praise you where they are as-sem-bled.

cresc.

"You who fear the Lord give him praise; all child-ren of Ja-cob, give him glo-ry. Re-vere him, *mf*

FINAL REFRAIN: *p* *Fine*

child-ren of Is-rael." My God, my God, why have you for-sa-ken me?

p My God, my God, why have you for-sa-ken me?

pp

The Lord Is My Light And My Help

Psalm 27

Francesca Leftley

2. There is one thing I ask___ of the Lord, for this I___ long, to

3. I am sure I shall see___ the Lord's good-ness in the land of the liv-ing.

live in the house___ of the Lord all the days of my life.___

Hope in him___ and take heart. Hope in the Lord.

Listen To The Voice Of The Lord

Psalm 95

Patrick Geary

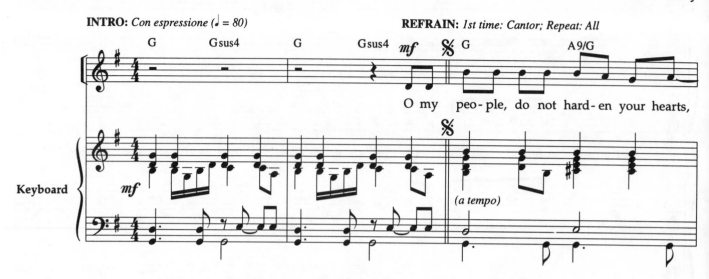

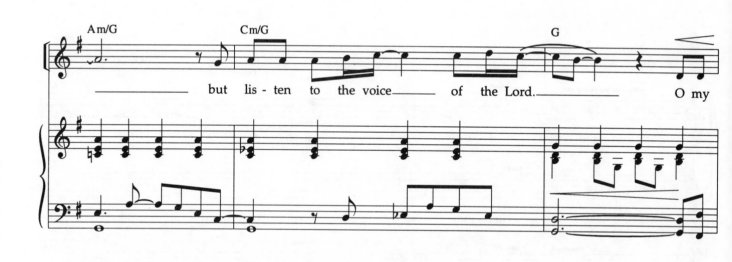

voice.

All: O my voice.

voice.

VERSE 1: *Cantor*

1. Come, sing out with joy to the Lord; praise the God who saves us.

With thanks-giv - ing come be - fore the Lord, with

27

28

VERSE 3: *Cantor*

3. If, to-day,——— you should hear the Lord,———
do not hard-en your hearts——————— as your an-ces-tors did——— in the
de - sert, when they doubt-ed,——— though they saw God's work. O my

REFRAIN: *All*

D.S.

29

You, Lord, Have The Message Of Eternal Life

Psalm 19

David Ogden

INTRO: Moderato con rubato (♩ = 72)

REFRAIN: *1st time: Cantor/Choir; Repeat: All*

You, Lord,— have the mes-sage of e-ter-nal life.— life.— 1–3. The life. 4. They are

law— of the Lord is per-fect, it re-vives— the soul.— The—
pre-cepts of the Lord are right,— they glad-den the heart.— The com-
fear— of the Lord is ho-ly, a - bid-ing for ev-er.— The de-
more to be de-sired than gold,— than the pur-est of gold— and—

rule of the Lord is to be trust-ed, it gives wis-dom to the sim - ple.
mand of the Lord— is— clear. It gives light— to the eyes.—
crees of the Lord— are— truth and— all— of them just.—
sweet-er are they— than— hon - ey, than— hon - ey from the comb.—

Bless The Lord, My Soul

Psalm 103

Jacques Berthier

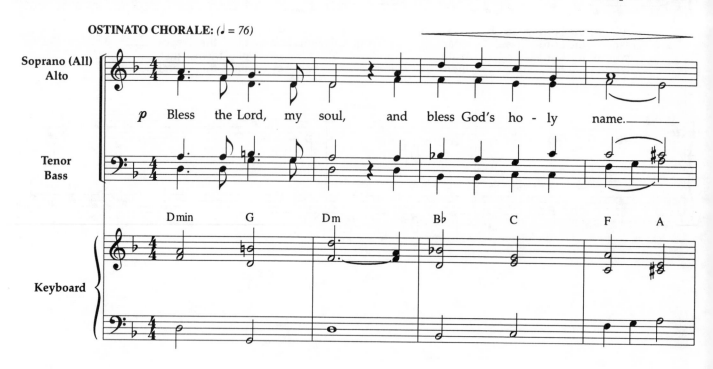

VERSE 1: *Cantor*

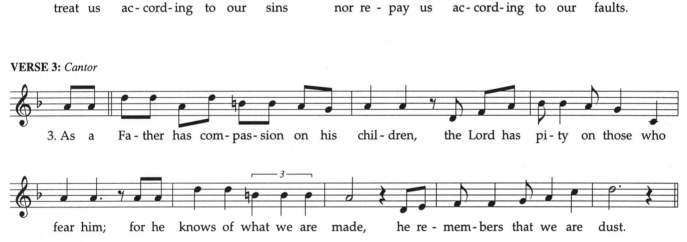

1. It is God who for-gives all your guilt, who heals ev-'ry one of your ills, who re-deems your life from the grave, who crowns you with love and com-pas-sion.

VERSE 2: *Cantor*

2. The Lord is com-pas-sion and love, slow to an-ger and rich in mer-cy. God does not treat us ac-cord-ing to our sins nor re-pay us ac-cord-ing to our faults.

VERSE 3: *Cantor*

3. As a Fa-ther has com-pas-sion on his chil-dren, the Lord has pi-ty on those who fear him; for he knows of what we are made, he re-mem-bers that we are dust.

My Shepherd Is The Lord

Psalm 23

John Glynn

Look Towards The Lord

for Laura Marie

Psalm 34

John Glynn

Look to-wards him.

1. I will al - ways
2. As you turn your
3. He sur-rounds you

bless the Lord,___ I will al - ways praise his name;___
eyes to him,___ you will find his eyes on you;___
with his love;___ he re - deems you from the grave;___

in the Lord my spir - it shall___ re - joice!
for he knows your need be - fore___ you ask!
you will taste the good - ness of___ the Lord!

37

From The Depths I Call To You

Psalm 130

Alan Smith

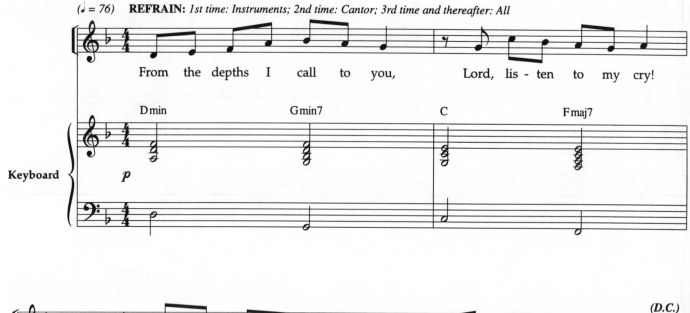

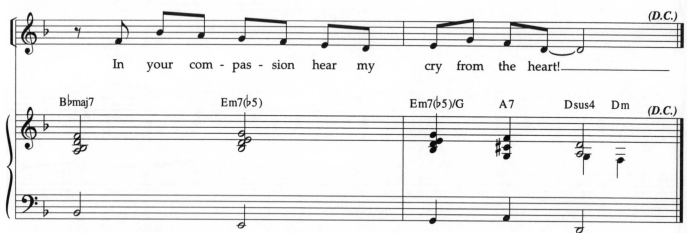

VERSES: *Cantor*

1. If you kept a re - cord of our sins, Lord, who could sur - vive?

2. I wait in hope for you, my God; I trust in your word.

3. It is with you that we find mer - cy and gen' - rous re - demp -

Dmin / Gmin7 / C / Fmaj7

_ But you for - give us, and for that we re - vere you. *D.C.*

_ As watch - ers long for dawn, so I yearn for you. *D.C.*

_ tion; you will save your peo - ple from all their sins. *D.C.*

B♭maj7 / Em7(♭5) / Em7(♭5)/G A7 Dsus4 Dm *D.C.*

The Blessing Cup

Psalm 116

Teresa Brown

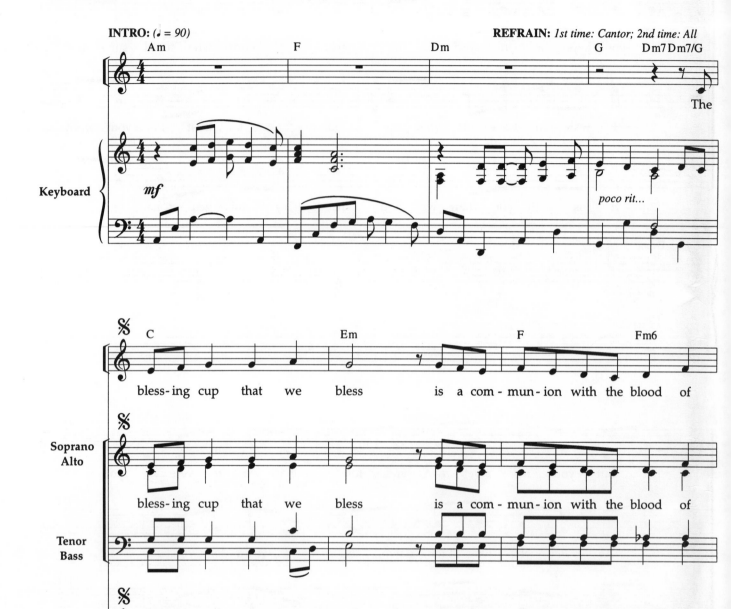

VERSES: *Cantor*

1. How can I re-pay the Lord for his good-ness to me?

2. O pre-cious in the eyes of the Lord is the death of his faith-ful.

3. A thanks-giv-ing sac-ri-fice I make: I will call on the Lord's name.

Nnn...

1. The cup of sal - va - tion I will raise; I will call on the Lord's name. The

2. Your ser - vant, Lord, your ser - vant am I; you have loos - ened my bonds. The

3. My vows to the Lord I will ful - fil be - fore all his peo - ple. The

(Nnn...)

The

poco rit...

REFRAIN: *All D.S.*

D.S.

Send Forth Your Spirit, O Lord

Psalm 104

Andrew Wright

VERSE 3: *Choir/Cantor*

44

May the Lord re-joice in his works, my thoughts be pleas-ing to him. I

VERSE 4: *Choir/Cantor*

find my joy in the Lord. 4. How man-y are your

works, O Lord! In wis-dom you have made them all. The earth is

full, is full of your rich-es, O Lord. Bless the Lord, O my soul.

45

Centre Of My Life

Psalm 16

Paul Inwood

46

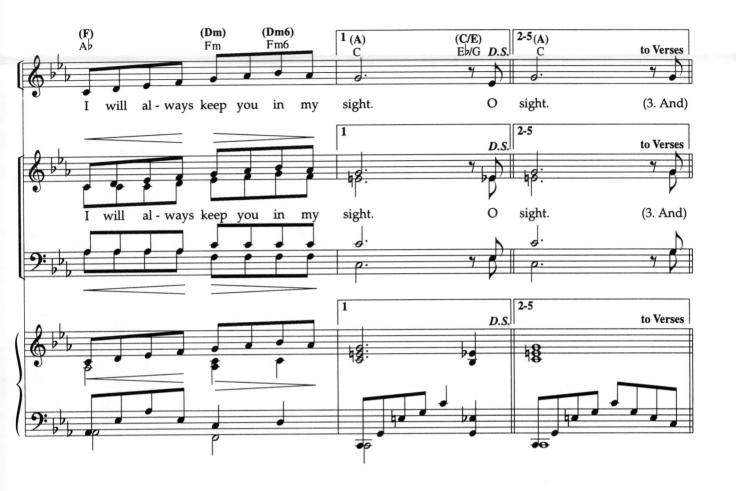

I will al-ways keep you in my sight. O sight. (3. And)

I will al-ways keep you in my sight. O sight. (3. And)

VERSE 1: *Cantor/Choir*

VERSE 2: *Cantor/Choir*

Lord, you are the cen-tre of my life: I will al-ways praise you,

Ah... Ah...

I will al-ways serve you, I will al-ways keep you in my sight.

rall.

pp

Canticle Of Moses

Exodus 15

John Gibbons

Performance note

At the start, the choir/cantor sings the first half of the refrain and the people join in with the second half.
Thereafter, the people sing both halves of the refrain, and the choir sopranos sing the descant.

glo - ri-ous___ in___ tri - umph.

glo - ri-ous___ in___ tri - umph.

VERSE 1: *Choir/Cantor*

1. Horse and ri - der   thrown to the sea!   The Lord is my   strength, my song, my sal-

va - tion.   This is my God, whom I___ ex - alt,   praise to my an - ces - tors' God.

2. The Lord is a war-rior, great his—name. The cha-riots of Pha-raoh hurled to the

sea. The might of his ar-my drowned in the sea.

Waves hide them, they sank like a stone.

VERSE 3: *Choir/Cantor*

3. Your right hand, Lord, is full of_ might; your right hand, Lord, has shat-tered the

en- e- my._____ Through the great-ness of_ your glo-ry you crushed the foe.

VERSE 4: *Choir/Cantor*

4. You will guide your peo-ple up to your moun-tain, the place, O Lord, where you make your

home. The shel-ter, Lord, your hands— have made. You will reign for e- ver and e- ver.

segue

FINAL REFRAIN:

I will sing to the Lord, sing to the Lord, glo- ri- ous— in—

Descant:

I will sing to the Lord, sing to the Lord, glo- ri- ous— in—

tri- umph.— I will sing to the Lord, sing to the Lord, glo- ri- ous— in— tri- umph.—

Fine

tri- umph.— I will sing to the Lord, sing to the Lord, glo- ri- ous— in— tri- umph.—

Fine

Fine

I Will Praise You

Psalm 30

Alan Smith

VERSES: *Cantor/Choir*

1. praise you, Lord,_____ you have res - cued me___ and have not let my en-e-mies re-

2. Sing psalms to the Lord, you who love___ him, give thanks to his

3. The Lord lis-tened and had pi - ty. The Lord_____

joice o-ver me.___ O Lord, you have raised my soul from the dead, re-stored me to

ho - ly name.___ His an-ger lasts a mo-ment; his fa-vour through life. At night there are

came to my help.___ For me you have changed my mourn-ing to danc-ing. Lord___ my

life from those___ who sink in - to the grave.

tears, at night there are tears, but joy comes with dawn.

God, I will thank you for ev - er, Lord my God.

REFRAIN: *All* D.S. I will

As The Deer Longs

Psalms 42 and 43

Bob Hurd
Arranged by Craig S Kingsbury

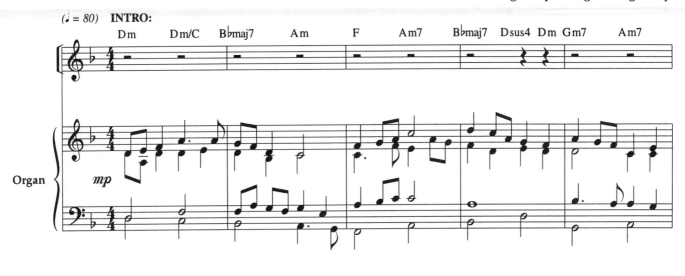

VERSES: *Choir*

1. A - thirst my soul_____ for you, the God who is my life!
2. ⁷ Ech - oes meet_____ as deep is call - ing un - to deep,
3. Con - tin - ual - ly_____ the foe de - lights in taunt - ing me:
4. De - fend me God,_____ send forth your light_____ and your truth,
5. Then I shall go_____ un - to the al - tar of my God.

Harmony

Concurrent Refrain (optional in verse 3)

As the deer longs for run - ning streams,

When shall I see, when shall I see, see the face of
o - ver my head, all your might - y wa - ters, sweep - ing o - ver
"Where is God, where is your God?" Where, O where are
they will lead me to your ho - ly moun - tain, to your dwell - ing
Prais - ing you, O my joy and glad - ness; I shall praise your

so I long, so I long, so I long for

God?
me.
you?
place.
name.

you.

63

Shout Joy To The Lord

Psalm 100

Ray d'Inverno

VERSES: *Cantor/Choir*

1. Shout joy to the Lord,___ all___ earth,___ serve the

2. Know that the Lord___ is___ God,___ our mak- er to

3. En- ter the tem- ple___ gates,___ the court- yard with

4. In- deed the Lord___ is___ good!___ God's

65

Lord— with— glad-ness,———— en - ter God's pre - sence with joy!— Shout

whom— we be - long,———— our shep-herd, and we— the— flock. Shout

thanks— and— praise;———— give thanks and bless— God's— name. Shout

love— is for ev - er, faith - ful from age— to— age.— Shout

joy to the Lord all earth.————

joy to the Lord all earth.————

joy to the Lord all earth.————

joy to the Lord all earth.————

66

Rejoice And Be Glad

Psalm 118

Patrick Geary

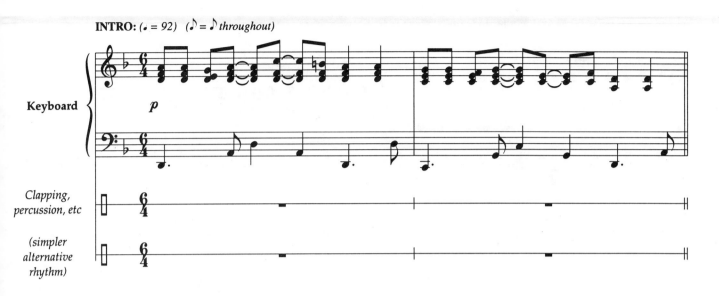

Performance note

After the introduction, the cantor should sing the first two bars of the refrain. Everyone joins in at the third bar. Thereafter, all sing the entire refrain throughout.

The piece may end with the refrain repeated several times. Vary the dynamic. The repeated refrain may fade to a whisper, or crescendo to a shout (in which case the small notes in the final bar may be used).

Clapping/percussion are only used in the refrain.

Last time to CODA ⊕

Al-le-lu-ia,— al - le-lu - ia! Al-le-lu-ia,— al - le-lu - ia!

Al-le-lu-ia,— al - le-lu - ia! Al-le-lu-ia,— al - le-lu - ia!

Last time to CODA ⊕

Last time to CODA ⊕

VERSES: *Cantor*

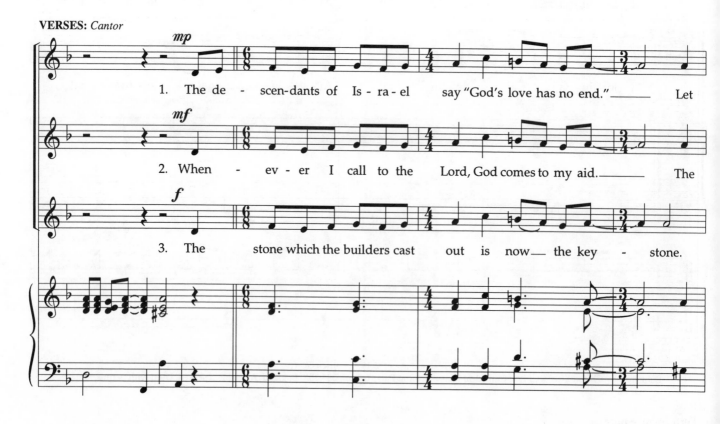

1. The de - scen-dants of Is - ra - el   say "God's love has no end."_____ Let

2. When - ev - er I call to the   Lord, God comes to my aid._____ The

3. The   stone which the builders cast   out is now— the key - stone.

all the world pro - claim: "God's love has no end";___ for all who love the

Lord is my strength, my song: God is my sal - va - tion. The just will shout for

How we mar - vel, Lord, at all you have done!___ This day was made by the

Lord know God's love won't end.

joy at the vic - t'ry of God.

Lord. Re - joice and be glad!

CODA:

Al - le - lu - ia,___ al - le - lu - ia!

Al - le - lu - ia,___ al - le - lu - ia!

The Lord Is My Shepherd

Psalm 23

Peter Ollis

Gently (♩. = 48)

REFRAIN: *1st time: Cantor/Choir; Repeat: All*

The Lord is my shep-herd; there is noth-ing I shall

(Soprano) The Lord is my shep-herd; there is noth-ing I shall

(Alto) The Lord is my shep-herd; there is noth-ing I shall

(Tenor) The Lord is my shep - herd; there is noth-ing I shall

(Bass) The Lord is my shep - herd; there is noth-ing I shall

REFRAIN: *All mf D.S.*

Fresh and green are the pas - tures where he gives me re - pose._____ The

REFRAIN: *All mf D.S.*

guides me a - long the right path; he is true to his name._____ The

D.S.

VERSE 3: *Cantor*

p

You have pre-pared_____ a ban - quet for me_____ in the sight of my foes. My

head you have a - noin-ted_____ with oil;_____ my cup is o - ver-flow-ing._____

72

Sure-ly good - ness and kind - ness shall fol - low me all the

days_____ of my life._____ In the Lord's own

house shall I dwell for ev - er and ev - er._____ The

FINAL REFRAIN: *All*

I Will Praise Your Name

Psalm 145

David Haas

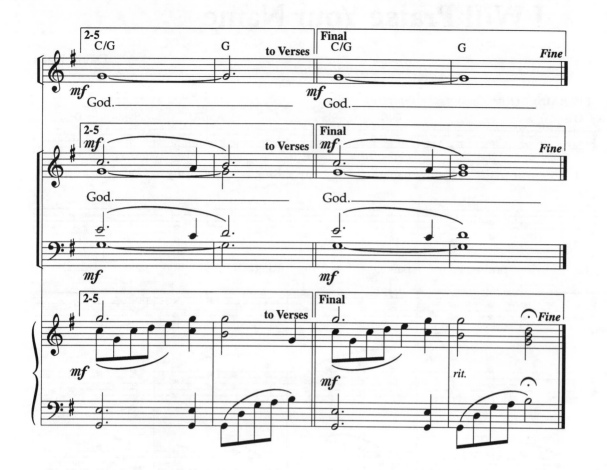

VERSES: *Choir/Cantor*

1. I will give you glo - ry my God and King, and I will bless___ your
2. The___ Lord is full of grace and mer - cy, he is kind___ and
3. Let___ all your works give you thanks O Lord, and let all___ the
4. The___ Lord is faith - ful in all his works, and al - ways near,___ his

Shout With Joy

Psalm 66

Alan Smith

(♩ = c.72) **REFRAIN:** *1st time: Choir/Cantor; Repeat: All*

Shout with joy to God, all earth! Sing the glo - ry of the Name!

Organ

VERSES: *Cantor/Choir*

Psalm 66

All earth, shout with **joy** to God!
Sing the glory **of** the Name!
Give **glo**rious praise!
Say, "How awe**some** your works!"

All earth **bows** before you,
sings to you, sings **to** your name.
Come, **see** God's wonders,
tremendous deeds **for** the people.

God turned sea **into** land,
they crossed the ri**ver** on foot.
Let us rejoice **then** in God,
who rules for ev**er** with might.

Come, listen, all **who** fear God,
as I tell what hap**pened** to me.
Bless God **who** did listen,
heeded the sound **of** my prayer.

A Blare Of Trumpets

Psalm 47

Paul Inwood

Final

Fine

for the Lord.

Final   *non rit.*   **Fine**

VERSE 1: *Cantor*

1. All peo-ples, clap your hands,   cry to God with shouts of

ritmico

joy!   For the Lord, the Most High,___ the   Lord, the Most High,___ we must

D.S.

fear,___   great   king o-ver all___ the   earth.

D.S.

80

2. God goes up with shouts of joy;   the Lord goes up with trum-pet

3. God is king of all the earth.   Sing praise with all your

ritmico

blast.   Sing praise to our God,____ sing praise to our God,____ sing

skill.   For the Lord____ is king,____ the Lord____ is king____ of all the

praise,_____ sing praise to our God,__ sing praise.

na - tions;   God reigns on his ho - ly throne.

D.S.

81

God's Love Is For Ever!

Psalm 136

Alan Smith

2. A - lone____ the mak - er of worlds!
3. Set the great____ lights____ a - bove!
4. Re - mem - bered____ our____ dis - tress!

God's love is for ev - er!____ Ar - chi - tect____ for the skies!
The sun to____ rule____ the day!
Kept us____ from____ de - feat!

God's love is for ev - er!____

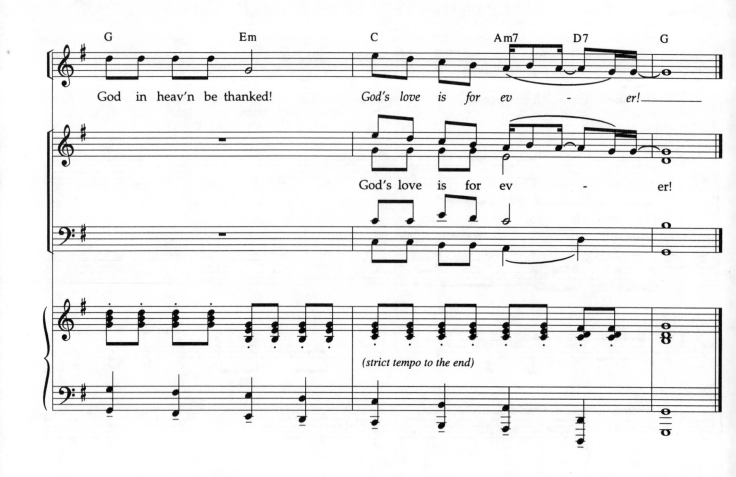

God in heav'n be thanked! *God's love is for ev - er!*

God's love is for ev - er!

(strict tempo to the end)

Blessed Be The Lord

Psalm 28

Ray d'Inverno

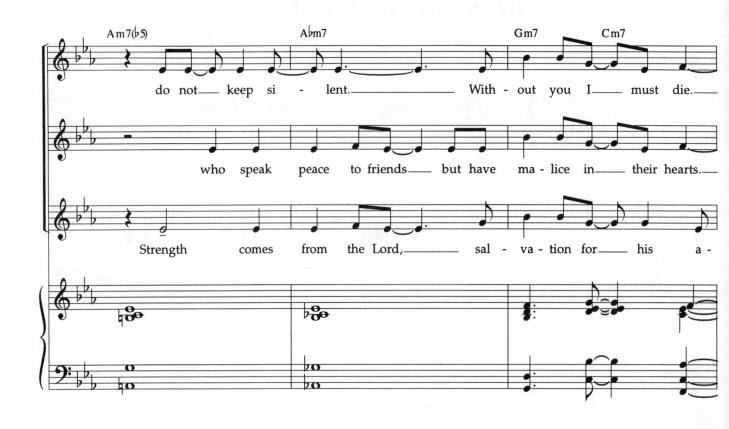

VERSE 3: *Cantor/Choir*

3. The ways of the Lord mean noth-ing to them.

May God de-stroy their world and nev - er re-build it.

91

God is the strong— shield——— in whom my heart— trusts.———

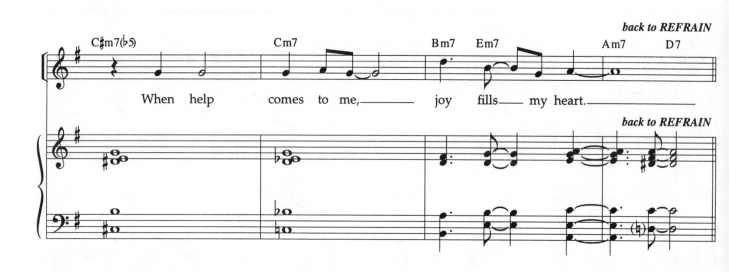

back to REFRAIN

When help comes to me,——— joy fills— my heart.———

back to REFRAIN

CODA:

the Lord who hears my cry.——————————— Bless- ed be the Lord,—

the Lord who hears my cry.——————————— Bless- ed be the Lord,—

The Lord Is King

Psalm 93

Paul Wellicome

VERSES: *Choir/Cantor*

Faster! (♩ = 180)

1. The Lord our king is clothed with ma - jes - ty,___ the
2. The world you found - ed, nev - er to be moved,___ the
k. The floods have lift - ed, lift - ed up, O Lord,___ the
4. The Lord is great - er than the great - est storm, more
5. Your words of wis - dom are so ve - ry sure.___

1. Lord_____ is__ clothed_____ with strength,_____
2. world_____ cre - at - ed firm._____
3. wa - ters lift - ed__ up_____ their voice._____
4. glo - rious than__ the_____ rag - ing of__ the seas._____
5. Ho - li - ness__ be - comes_____ your house._____

1. the Lord_____ our king wears pow - er_____ for a crown. Lord,
2. Your throne_____ es - tab - lished, nev - er_____ to be moved. Lord,
3. The o - ceans thun - dered, thun - dered_____ out their might: Lord,
4. The Lord__ is might - ier than their_____ thun - dered might! Lord,
5. Sure - ly your de - crees are nev - er_____ in dis - pute? Lord,

you reign_____ for ev - er - more._____
you reign_____ for ev - er - more._____
you reign_____ for ev - er - more._____
you reign_____ for ev - er - more._____
you reign_____ for ev - er - more._____

Lord, Take Up My Cause

(Psalm for the unborn child)

Psalms 138 and 139

Peter Ollis

REFRAIN: *1st time: Cantor; Repeat: All*

Lord, take up my cause; Lord, your love lasts for ev - er.

Do not a-ban-don me; Lord, do not a-ban-don what your hands___ have made.

hands— have made. hands— have made.

VERSE 1: *Cantor*

1. You cre - at - ed ev'-ry part of me, knit - ting me in my moth-er's

womb. For such hand - i-work I praise— you. Awe - some

this great won-der! I see it so clear-ly._____

2. You, you watched ev'-ry bone tak-ing shape, tak-ing shape___ in se-cret, form-ing in the hid-den depths. You saw my bod-y grow ac-cord-ing to your de - sign.

99

God Goes Up

Psalm 47

Teresa Brown

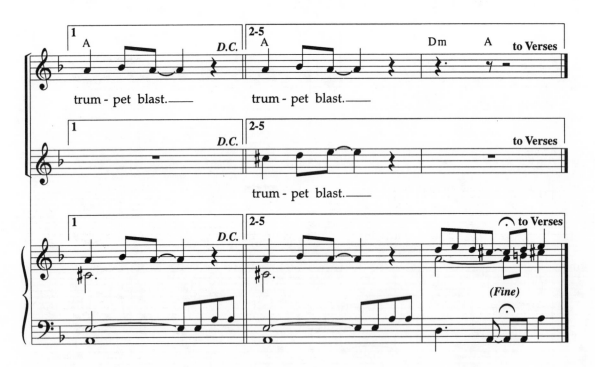

1. All peoples,— clap your hands,— cry to God with shouts of joy!—

2. God goes up with shouts of joy;— the Lord goes up with trum-pet blast.—

3. God is king of all the earth.— Sing praise with all your skill.—

mf

For the Lord, the most high, we must fear, great king o-ver all the earth.—

Sing praise for God, sing praise,— sing praise to our king, sing praise.—

God is king o-ver the na-tions; God reigns on his ho-ly throne.—

D.C.

101

Father, Into Your Hands

Psalm 31

Plainchant, arr. G Boulton Smith

REFRAIN: *1st time: Cantor; Repeat: All*

Fa - ther, in - to your hands I com - mend my —— spi - rit.

Cantor:

Psalm 31

In you, O Lord, **I** take refuge.
Let me never be **put** to shame.
In your justice set me free. Into your hands I com**mend** my spirit.
It is you who will re**deem** me, Lord.

In the face of **all** my foes
I am **a** reproach,
an object of scorn **to** my neighbours
and of fear **to** my friends.

Those who see me **in** the street
run far **away** from me.
I am like a dead man, forgotten **in** men's hearts,
like a thing **thrown** away.

But as for me, I **trust** in you, Lord,
I say: "You **are** my God."
My life is in your **hands,** deliver me
from the hands of **those** who hate me.

Let your face shine **on** your servant,
save me **in** your love.
Be strong, let your **heart** take courage,
all who hope **in** the Lord.

Rest Your Love

FLUTE

David Ogden

The Lord Is My Light And My Help

C INSTRUMENT I

Francesca Leftley

C INSTRUMENT II

Francesca Leftley

CELLO/ELECTRIC BASS

Francesca Leftley

Listen To The Voice Of The Lord

TREBLE INSTRUMENTS I & II

Patrick Geary

CELLO

Patrick Geary

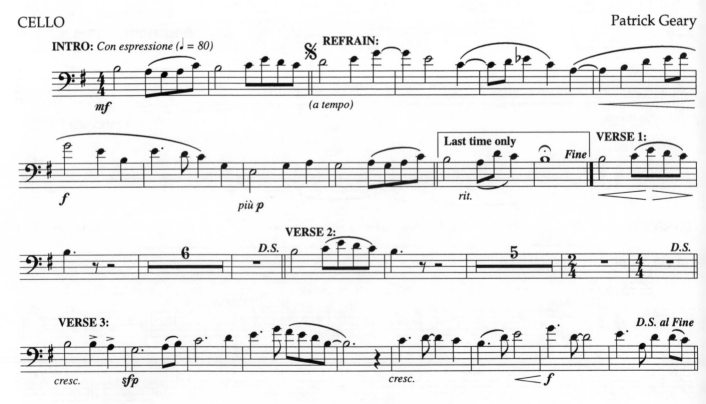

You, Lord, Have The Message Of Eternal Life

FLUTE

David Ogden

Bless The Lord, My Soul

C INSTRUMENT (Simple melody)

Jacques Berthier

BASSOON

Jacques Berthier

105

Bless The Lord, My Soul

RECORDER DUO

Jacques Berthier

FLUTE DUO

Jacques Berthier

B♭ TRUMPET

Jacques Berthier

From The Depths I Call To You

VIOLIN I

Alan Smith

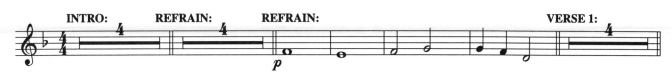

VIOLIN II

Alan Smith

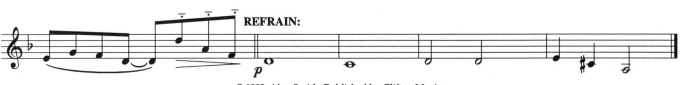

From The Depths I Call To You

VIOLA

Alan Smith

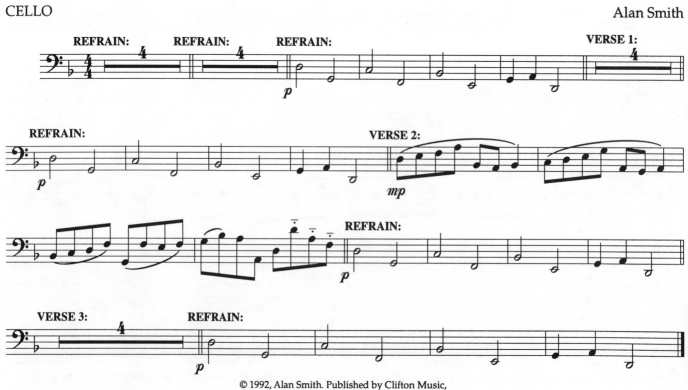

CELLO

Alan Smith

Send Forth Your Spirit, O Lord

C INSTRUMENTS I & II

Andrew Wright

PERCUSSION

Andrew Wright

Centre Of My Life

SOLO INSTRUMENT I

Paul Inwood

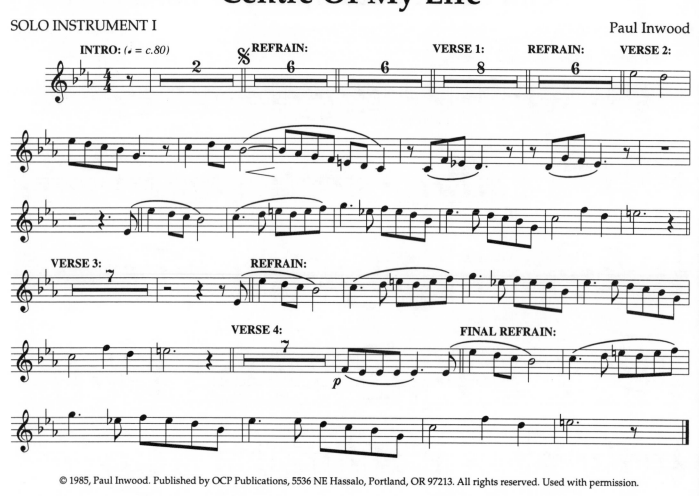

SOLO INSTRUMENT II

Paul Inwood

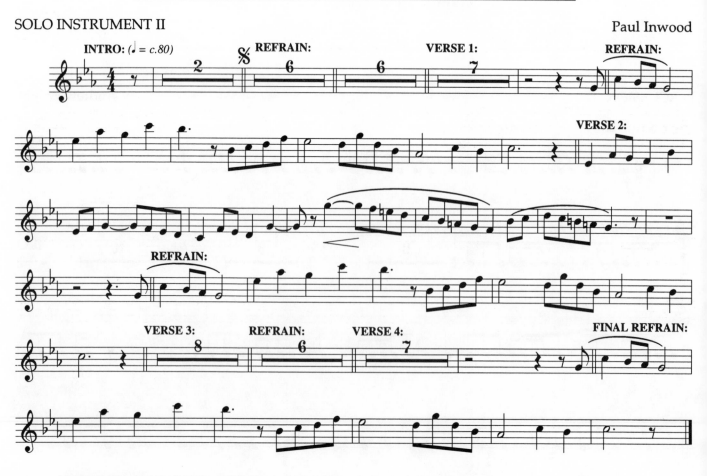

As The Deer Longs

SOLO INSTRUMENT I Craig S Kingsbury

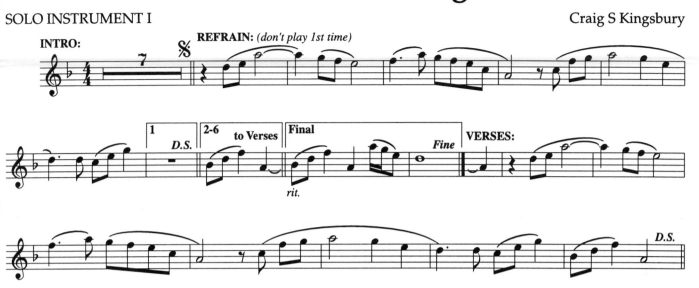

SOLO INSTRUMENT II Craig S Kingsbury

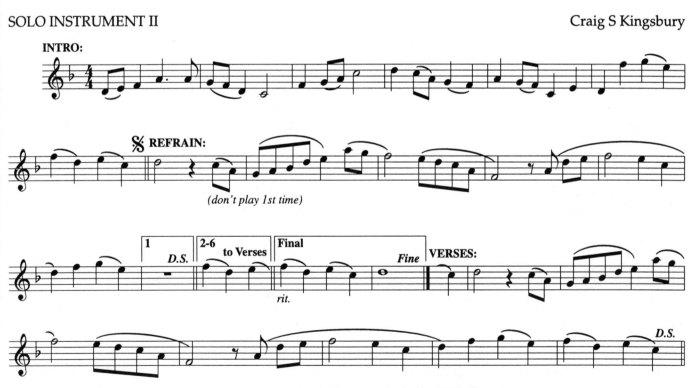

Canticle Of Moses

FLUTE

John Gibbons

112

Canticle Of Moses

OBOE

John Gibbons

Canticle Of Moses

B♭ TRUMPET

John Gibbons

Canticle Of Moses

BASS

John Gibbons

A Blare Of Trumpets

Paul Inwood

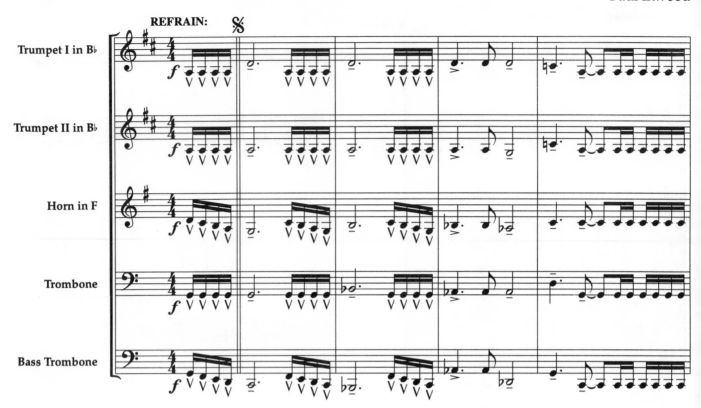

Final

Fine **VERSES**

D.S.

Refrains

Psalm 51 — I WILL LEAVE THIS PLACE — Paul Wellicome

I will leave this place and re - turn to my fa-ther's house, my fa-ther's house.

Psalm 51 — O LORD, YOU LOVE SINCERITY OF HEART — Elizabeth Rees

O Lord, you love sin-cer-i-ty of heart.

Teach me the se - crets of wis - dom.

Psalm 91 — SONG OF BLESSING — John Glynn

May the Lord bless you, may he lay his hand up -

on you, and keep you as the ap-ple of his eye:_____

— may his love pro - tect you, may he guard you from all

e - vil, and Je-sus be the Way you trav-el by._____

Psalm 33 — REST YOUR LOVE — David Ogden

O Lord, gent - ly rest your love.

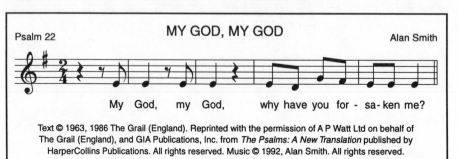

Psalm 22 — MY GOD, MY GOD — Alan Smith

My God, my God, why have you for - sa-ken me?

For permission to photocopy, see page 2.

118

LORD, HOW CAN I REPAY

John Glynn

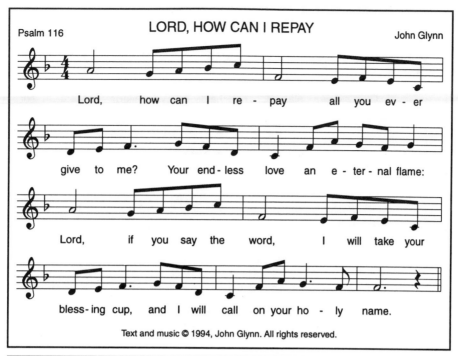

Lord, how can I re-pay all you ev-er give to me? Your end-less love an e-ter-nal flame: Lord, if you say the word, I will take your bless-ing cup, and I will call on your ho-ly name.

BY THE WATERS OF BABYLON

Traditional

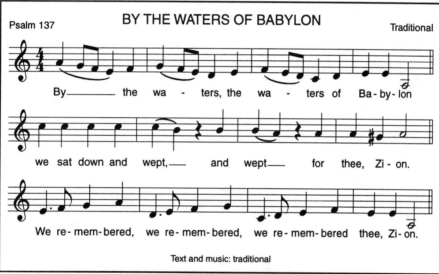

By the wa-ters, the wa-ters of Ba-by-lon we sat down and wept,— and wept— for thee, Zi-on. We re-mem-bered, we re-mem-bered, we re-mem-bered thee, Zi-on.

Text and music: traditional

THE LORD IS MY LIGHT AND MY HELP

Francesca Leftley

The Lord is my light and my help.— The Lord is my light— and my help.

YOU, LORD, HAVE THE MESSAGE OF ETERNAL LIFE

David Ogden

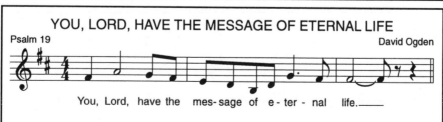

You, Lord, have the mes-sage of e-ter-nal life.—

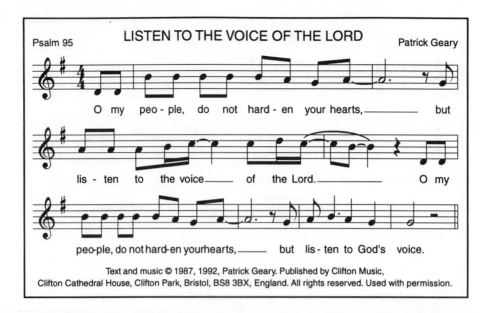

LISTEN TO THE VOICE OF THE LORD

Psalm 95 — Patrick Geary

O my peo - ple, do not hard - en your hearts, ———— but lis - ten to the voice ——— of the Lord. ——— O my peo-ple, do not hard-en your hearts, ——— but lis - ten to God's voice.

BLESS THE LORD, MY SOUL

Psalm 103 — Jacques Berthier

Bless the Lord, my soul, and bless God's ho - ly name. Bless the Lord, my soul, who leads me in - to life.

MY SHEPHERD IS THE LORD

Psalm 23 — John Glynn

My shep - herd is the Lord; he is ev' - ry - thing, ev' - ry - thing. —— My shep - herd is the Lord; he is ev' - ry - thing, ——— ev' - ry - thing ——— to me.

LOOK TOWARDS THE LORD

Psalm 34 — John Glynn

Look to - wards the Lord, keep your eyes on him, and you will be filled with his light.

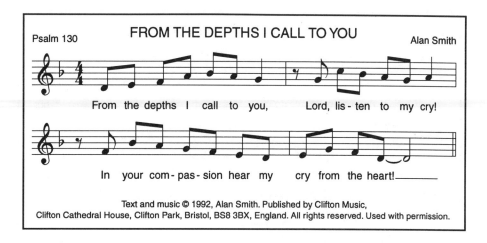

Psalm 130

FROM THE DEPTHS I CALL TO YOU

Alan Smith

From the depths I call to you, Lord, lis-ten to my cry!

In your com-pas-sion hear my cry from the heart!_____

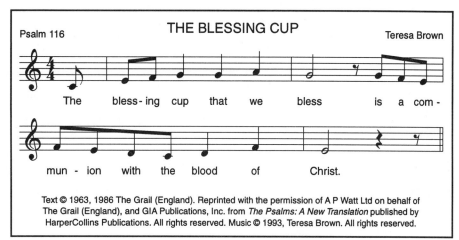

Psalm 116

THE BLESSING CUP

Teresa Brown

The bless-ing cup that we bless is a com-

mun-ion with the blood of Christ.

Psalm 104

SEND FORTH YOUR SPIRIT, O LORD

Andrew Wright

Send forth, send forth your Spir-it, O

Lord,_____ and re-new_____ the face of the earth.

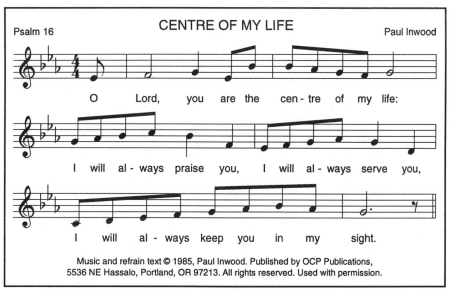

Psalm 16

CENTRE OF MY LIFE

Paul Inwood

O Lord, you are the cen-tre of my life:

I will al-ways praise you, I will al-ways serve you,

I will al-ways keep you in my sight.

For permission to photocopy, see page 2.

CANTICLE OF MOSES

Exodus 15

John Gibbons

I will sing to the Lord, sing to the Lord, glo-ri-ous— in— tri-umph.— I will sing to the Lord, sing to the Lord, glo-ri-ous— in— tri-umph.—

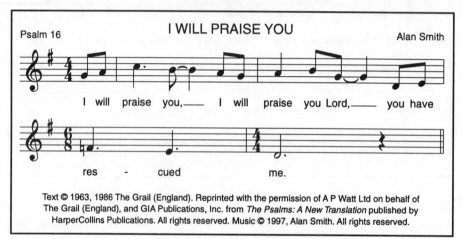

I WILL PRAISE YOU

Psalm 16

Alan Smith

I will praise you,— I will praise you Lord,— you have res - cued me.

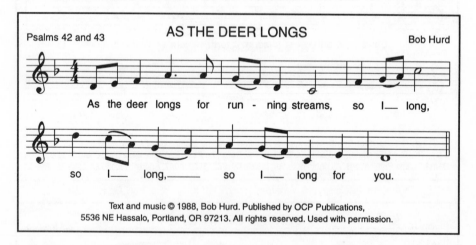

AS THE DEER LONGS

Psalms 42 and 43

Bob Hurd

As the deer longs for run - ning streams, so I— long, so I— long,— so I— long for you.

REJOICE AND BE GLAD

Psalm 118

Patrick Geary

Al-le-lu-ia,— al-le-lu-ia! Al-le-lu-ia,— al-le-lu-ia! Al-le-lu-ia,— al-le-lu-ia! Al-le-lu-ia,— al-le-lu-ia!

Psalm 100

SHOUT JOY TO THE LORD

Ray d'Inverno

Shout joy to the Lord, shout joy to the Lord, shout joy to the Lord all earth. Shout joy to the Lord, shout joy to the Lord, shout joy to the Lord all earth.

Psalm 23

THE LORD IS MY SHEPHERD

Peter Ollis

The Lord is my shepherd; there is noth-ing I shall want

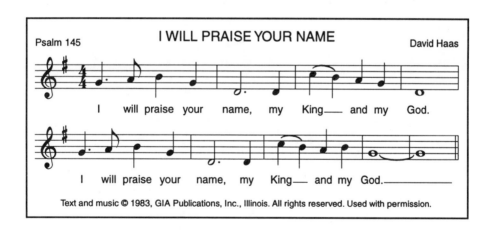

Psalm 145

I WILL PRAISE YOUR NAME

David Haas

I will praise your name, my King and my God. I will praise your name, my King and my God.

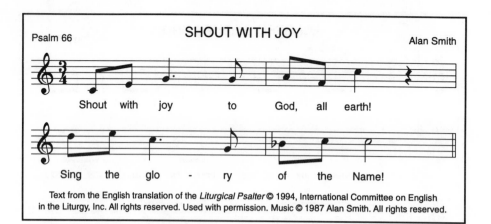

SHOUT WITH JOY

Psalm 66

Alan Smith

Shout with joy to God, all earth!

Sing the glo - ry of the Name!

A BLARE OF TRUMPETS

Psalm 47

Paul Inwood

God mounts his throne to shouts of joy:

a blare of trum - pets for the Lord.____

GOD'S LOVE IS FOR EVER!

Psalm 136

Alan Smith

(Cantor)   (All)

God's love is for ev - er!____

God's love is for ev - er!____

God's love is for ev - er!

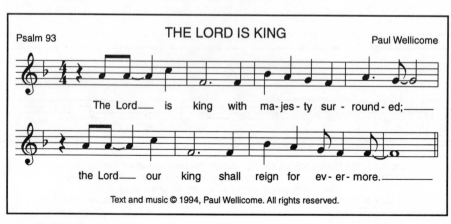

THE LORD IS KING

Psalm 93

Paul Wellicome

The Lord__ is king with ma - jes - ty sur - round - ed;__

the Lord__ our king shall reign for ev - er - more.__

BLESSED BE THE LORD

Psalm 28   Ray d'Inverno

Bless-ed be the Lord,_____ bless-ed be the Lord,_

_____ bless-ed be the Lord,

the Lord who hears my cry._

LORD, TAKE UP MY CAUSE

Psalm 138/139   Peter Ollis

Lord, take up my cause; Lord, your love lasts for

ev - er. Do not a - ban - don me;

Lord, do not a - ban - don what your hands___ have made.

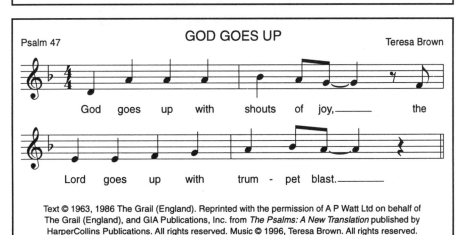

GOD GOES UP

Psalm 47   Teresa Brown

God goes up with shouts of joy,_____ the

Lord goes up with trum - pet blast._

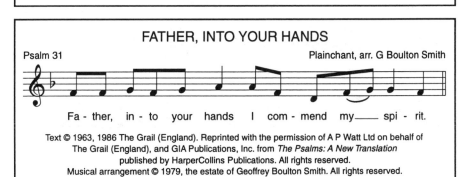

FATHER, INTO YOUR HANDS

Psalm 31   Plainchant, arr. G Boulton Smith

Fa - ther, in - to your hands I com - mend my___ spi - rit.

Topical Index

Common Psalms

Roman Lectionary

Liturgical Index
Revised Common Lectionary

Liturgical Index
Roman Lectionary